Personal message from Elaine Nembhard, the Creator of the Soci

Thank you for purchasing this product from us. We hope you find it useful and will take the time to explore the range of products that we have produced to help you to "work smarter" instead of "harder."

As you are the ones we hope will use the product, we value your comments so any feedback you can give to improve the benefits of this product or any other of our note pads, would be welcomed.

We also invite you to contact us with any ideas you have about creating a cost effective product that would be helpful to our profession so we can work together to make it happen.

We hope that you will try the other products in this range and if you need to get in touch our details are below. If you wish to contact us you can do so via our website at www.maydaysocialworkconsultancy.co.uk

Please note, this notebook is **NOT** a guide on how to conduct assessments but if followed through, it will help to focus on the type of information that needs to be gathered.

PERSONAL NOTES

USEFUL BACKGROUND NOTES

Our assessment workbook is not a comprehensive guide to child and family assessment. It merely aims to provide practitioners with some guidance to focus and record information for their assessments. The structure of the workbook makes use of the various frameworks and approaches already familiar to practitioners including evidence-based issues known to negatively influence a child's holistic wellbeing.

SAFEGUARDING: LEGAL FRAMEWORK REFERENCE

'Child protection' or 'safeguarding' in the United Kingdom is governed by different pieces of legislation. Over the years, these have been revised or replaced. The most enduring legislation for safeguarding work has been The Children's Act 1989. At the heart of the Act, is the emphasis on the care, protection and the welfare of children up to their 18th birthday. Critically the Act defines parental responsibility.

It promotes working in partnership with parents and encouraged interagency collaboration. Significant changes were introduced by The Children Act 2004. It sets out the legal basis for how social services and others deal with matters relating to the children they are looking after regardless of whether it is in the home, school or elsewhere. Below are sections of The Children Act 1989 that is frequently called upon in child protection or safeguarding:

Section 1	Paramountcy Principle
Section 17	Provision of Services for Children in Need
Section 47	Duty to Investigate
Section 46	Police Powers
Section 44	Emergency Protection Powers
Section 20	Co-operative Agreement into Care
Section 31	Care Orders
Section 3	Parental Responsibility

The Children Act 2004

The Children Act 2004 did not replace or amend much of the Children Act 1989 instead it introduced significant changes for child protection or safeguarding arrangements and functions. For example, it

- Places a duty on local authorities and partners (including the police, health service providers and the youth justice system) to co-operate in promoting the wellbeing of children and young people and to make arrangements to safeguard and promote the welfare of children.

References: Working Together to Safeguard Children
https://assets.publishing.service.gov.uk/government/uploads/system/uploads/attachment_data/file/7794
01/Working_Together_to_Safeguard-Children.pdf
Children Act 1989   https://www.legislation.gov.uk/ukpga/1989/41/contents
Children Act 2004   http://www.legislation.gov.uk/ukpga/2004/31/notes/division/1/1

SOME USEFUL DEFINITIONS

1. **Children: Anyone who has not yet reached their 18th birthday**

   The fact that a child has reached 16 years of age, is living independently or is in further education, is a member of the armed forces, is in hospital or custody in the secure estate, does not change their status or entitlements to services or protection.

2. **Safeguarding and promoting the welfare of children**

   Defined for this guidance as:

   a) protecting children from maltreatment

   b) preventing impairment of children's health or development

   c) ensuring that children are growing up in the circumstances consistent with the provision of safe and effective care

   d) taking action to enable all children to have the best outcomes

3. **Child protection - Part of safeguarding and promoting welfare**

   This refers to the activity that is undertaken to protect specific children who are suffering, or are likely to suffer, significant harm.

4. **Abuse: A form of maltreatment of a child**

   Somebody may abuse or neglect a child by inflicting harm, or by failing to act to prevent harm. Children may be abused in a family or an institutional or community setting by those known to them or, more rarely, by others. Abuse can take place wholly online, or technology may be used to facilitate offline abuse. Children may be abused by an adult or adults, or another child or children.

5. **Physical abuse**

   A form of abuse which may involve hitting, shaking, throwing, poisoning, burning or scalding, drowning, suffocating or otherwise causing physical harm to a child. Physical harm may also be caused when a parent or carer fabricates the symptoms of or deliberately induces, illness in a child.

6. **Emotional abuse**

   The persistent emotional maltreatment of a child such as to cause severe and persistent adverse effects on the child's emotional development. It may involve conveying to a child that they are worthless or unloved, inadequate, or valued only insofar as they meets the needs of another person. It may include not giving the child opportunities to express their views, deliberately silencing them or 'making fun' of what they say or how they communicate. It may feature age or developmentally inappropriate expectations being imposed on children. These may include interactions that are beyond a child's developmental capability, as well as overprotection and limitation of exploration and learning, or preventing the child participating in normal social interaction. It may involve seeing or hearing the ill-treatment of another. It may involve serious bullying (including cyberbullying), causing children frequently to feel frightened or in danger, or the exploitation or corruption of children. Some level of emotional abuse is involved in all types of maltreatment of a child, though it may occur alone.

7. **Sexual abuse**

Involves forcing or enticing a child or young person to take part in sexual activities, not necessarily involving a high level of violence, whether or not the child is aware of what is happening. The activities may involve physical contact, including assault by penetration (for example, rape or oral sex) or non-penetrative acts such as masturbation, kissing, rubbing and touching outside of clothing. They may also include non-contact activities, such as involving children in looking at, or in the production of, sexual images, watching sexual activities, encouraging children to behave in sexually inappropriate ways, or grooming a child in preparation for abuse Sexual abuse can take place online, and technology can be used to facilitate offline abuse. Sexual abuse is not solely perpetrated by adult males. Women can also commit acts of sexual abuse, as can other children.

8. **Child sexual exploitation**

Child sexual exploitation is a form of child sexual abuse. It occurs where an individual or group takes advantage of an imbalance of power to coerce, manipulate or deceive a child or young person under the age of 18 into sexual activity (a) in exchange for something the victim needs or wants, and/or (b) for the financial advantage or increased status of the perpetrator or facilitator. The victim may have been sexually exploited even if the sexual activity appears consensual. Child sexual exploitation does not always involve physical contact; it can also occur through the use of technology.

9. **Neglect**

The persistent failure to meet a child's basic physical and psychological needs, likely to result in the serious impairment of the child's health or development. Neglect may occur during pregnancy as a result of maternal substance abuse. Once a child is born, neglect may involve a parent or carer failing to:

a)   provide adequate food, clothing and shelter (including exclusion from home or abandonment)

b)   protect a child from physical and emotional harm or danger

c)   ensure adequate supervision (including the use of inadequate caregivers)

d)   ensure access to appropriate medical care or treatment

e)   It may also include neglect of, or unresponsiveness to, a child's basic emotional needs.

10. **Extremism**

Extremism goes beyond terrorism and includes people who target the vulnerable – including the young – by seeking to sow division between communities on the basis of race, faith or denomination; justify discrimination towards women and girls; persuade others that minorities are inferior; or argue against the primacy of democracy and the rule of law in our society.

Extremism is defined in the Counter Extremism Strategy 2015 as the vocal or active opposition to our fundamental values, including the rule of law, individual liberty and the mutual respect and tolerance of different faiths and beliefs. We also regard calls for the death of members of our armed forces as extremist.

11. **Young carer**

    A young carer is a person under 18 who provides or intends to provide care for another person (of any age, except generally where that care is provided for payment, under a contract or as voluntary work).

12. **Parent carer**

    A person aged 18 or over who provides or intends to provide care for a disabled child for whom the person has parental responsibility.

13. **Education, Health and Care Plan (EHCP)**

    A single plan, which covers the education, health and social care needs of a child or young person with special educational needs and disability (SEND). See the Special Educational Needs and Disability Code of Practice 0-25 (2014).

14. **Safeguarding partners**

    A safeguarding partner in relation to a local authority area in England is defined under the Children Act 2004 as
    a) the local authority
    b) a clinical commissioning group for an area any part of which falls within the local authority area, and
    c) the chief officer of police for an area any part of which falls within the local authority area.

    The three safeguarding partners should agree on ways to coordinate their safeguarding services; act as a strategic leadership group in supporting and engaging others, and implement local and national learning including from serious child safeguarding incidents. To fulfil this role, the three safeguarding partners must set out how they will work together and with any relevant agencies as well as arrangements for conducting local reviews.

15. **County Lines**

    As set out in the Serious Violence Strategy, published by the Home Office, a term used to describe gangs and organised criminal networks involved in exporting illegal drugs into one or more importing areas within the UK, using dedicated mobile phone lines or other forms of 'deal line'. They are likely to exploit children and vulnerable adults to move and store the drugs and money, and they will often use coercion, intimidation, violence (including sexual violence) and weapons.

16. **Child criminal exploitation**

   As set out in the Serious Violence Strategy, published by the Home Office, where an individual or group takes advantage of an imbalance of power to coerce, control, manipulate or deceive a child or young person under the age of 18 into any criminal activity

   a)   in exchange for something the victim needs or wants, and/or

   b)   for the financial or other advantage of the perpetrator or facilitator and/or

   c)   through violence or the threat of violence.

   The victim may have been criminally exploited even if the activity appears consensual. Child criminal exploitation does not always involve physical contact; it can also occur through the use of technology.

The above definitions are from Working Together to Safeguard Children A guide to inter-agency working to safeguard and promote the welfare of children July 2018 www.gov.uk/government/publications

ASSESSMENT FRAMEWORK

The assessment starts with gathering information and unless told otherwise the framework that is used for assessments is the [1]*Framework for Assessment of Children in Need and their Families* commonly called the triangle.

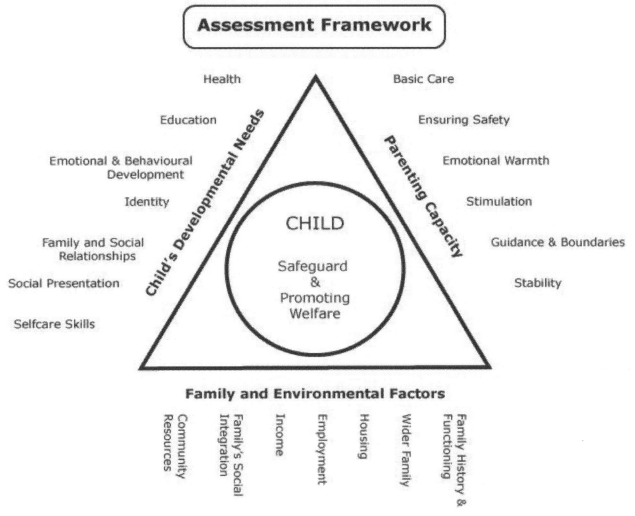

The triangle is a road map for collecting information about a child's developmental needs and factors that affect these need including parenting capacity and family and environmental influences. The explanatory notes for each heading are given below with additional notes of other areas to consider. There will be other influential factors not included in the triangle or our additions therefore practitioners will need to give this due consideration in the context of their assessments.

Remember the triangle is a road map to gather information and focus the assessment so use it and the note pad widely, making decisions as you go along about relevance of some information. Do not stick to it rigidly. Make it work for you to get you to where you need to go. Without following some kind of structure, you may end up with a less meaningful assessment.

---

[1] Department of Health, Department for Education and Employment and Home Office (2000)

Background - review the referral, management case directions, chronology, history of involvement and anything you feel will help you to understand the task ahead.

Section Two: The Initial or Assessment Home Visit

The first home visit to the family is your opportunity to collect significant facts about the family and get some of the formalities out of the way. In preparation for the visit, use the checklist below plus any other to make sure you have what you need. If there has been previous involvement, you might already have a genogram or ecomap for the family so take a copy with you to update it rather than starting from scratch.

Assessment explanatory notes		Consent form		Complaints procedure	
Direct work tools		Genogram		Eco Map	
Referral forms					

Demographics –If the family are known to the service or using the referral, make a note of the information you have for them and check with the family when you meet to make sure it is current and accurate.

Name		DOB		Gender		Disability	
Name		DOB		Gender		Disability	
Name		DOB		Gender		Disability	
Name		DOB		Gender		Disability	

Ethnicity	Language	Religion	Legal status

Further information (parental responsibility, child or parent with disability as identified by the service. Information about the family's *structure, culture, religion, ethnic origin* needs to be collected and analysed as the information could have significant bearing on their approach to parenting, child safety and impact the child.

Section Three: Explore the parents/carers/family's understanding of the concerns and the referral.

Section Four: Gathering and analysing the information for each child

 This section allows you to gather information for about four children, so you may have to use copy pages if you need more). Information gathering should focus on strengths as well as difficulties.   You can separate the areas below as appropriate.

(1) Health
(2) Education
(3) Emotional and Behavioural Development
(4) Identity
(5)   Social Relationships
(6) Self-care skills
(7) Social presentation

Section Five: Parenting Capacity

This includes evidence of direct observations supplemented by information from other professionals, discussions parents and direct work and discussions with the child/ren.   Include analysis of strengths, difficulties and unmet needs – what if *anything is having a negative or positive impact on the child/ren.*

(1) Basic care
(2) Ensuring safety
(3)   Emotional warmth
(4) Stimulation
(5) Guidance and Boundaries
(6)   Stability

Section Six: Family and environmental factors

This section should include evidence from own observations and other sources. Consider adults in the home and around the child/ren who are considered to be or likely to be posting a risk of significant harm to the child/ren. Again topics can be combined or separated

(1) Family History and Functioning
(2) Wider Family and Significant Others
(3) Housing, Employment and Income
(4) Family's social integration/community resources
(5) Any current/historical social care involvement/services from other agencies

Continuation of Section Six: Family and Environmental Factors

Section Seven: Views of All Parties

Section Eight: Risks and Protective Factors

Section One: Preparation

Background - review the referral, management case directions, chronology, history of involvement and anything you feel will help you to understand the task ahead.

Section Two: The Initial or Assessment Home Visit

The first home visit to the family is your opportunity to collect significant facts about the family and get some of the formalities out of the way. In preparation for the visit, use the checklist below plus any other to make sure you have what you need. If there has been previous involvement, you might already have a genogram or ecomap for the family so take a copy with you to update it rather than starting from scratch.

Assessment explanatory notes		Consent form		Complaints procedure	
Direct work tools		Genogram		Eco Map	
Referral forms					

Demographics –If the family are known to the service or using the referral, make a note of the information you have for them and check with the family when you meet to make sure it is current and accurate.

Name		DOB		Gender		Disability	
Name		DOB		Gender		Disability	
Name		DOB		Gender		Disability	
Name		DOB		Gender		Disability	

Ethnicity	Language	Religion	Legal status

Further information (parental responsibility, child or parent with disability as identified by the service. Information about the family's *structure, culture, religion, ethnic origin* needs to be collected and analysed as the information could have significant bearing on their approach to parenting, child safety and impact the child.

Section Three: Explore the parents/carers/family's understanding of the concerns and the referral.

Section Four: Gathering and analysing the information for each child

This section allows you to gather information for about four children, so you may have to use copy pages if you need more). Information gathering should focus on strengths as well as difficulties.   You can separate the areas below as appropriate.

(1) Health
(2) Education
(3) Emotional and Behavioural Development
(4) Identity
(5)   Social Relationships
(6) Self-care skills
(7) Social presentation

Continuation of Section Four: Gathering and analysing the information for each child

Section Five: Parenting Capacity

This includes evidence of direct observations supplemented by information from other professionals, discussions parents and direct work and discussions with the child/ren.   Include analysis of strengths, difficulties and unmet needs – what if *anything is having a negative or positive impact on the child/ren.*

(1) Basic care
(2) Ensuring safety
(3)   Emotional warmth
(4) Stimulation
(5) Guidance and Boundaries
(6)   Stability

Continuation of Section Five: Parenting Capacity

Continuation of Section Five: Parenting Capacity

Section Six: Family and environmental factors

This section should include evidence from own observations and other sources. Consider adults in the home and around the child/ren who are considered to be or likely to be posting a risk of significant harm to the child/ren. Again topics can be combined or separated

(1) Family History and Functioning
(2) Wider Family and Significant Others
(3) Housing, Employment and Income
(4) Family's social integration/community resources
(5) Any current/historical social care involvement/services from other agencies

Continuation of Section Six: Family and Environmental Factors

Section Seven: Views of All Parties

Section Eight: Risks and Protective Factors

Section One: Preparation

Background - review the referral, management case directions, chronology, history of involvement and anything you feel will help you to understand the task ahead.

Section Two: The Initial or Assessment Home Visit

The first home visit to the family is your opportunity to collect significant facts about the family and get some of the formalities out of the way. In preparation for the visit, use the checklist below plus any other to make sure you have what you need. If there has been previous involvement, you might already have a genogram or ecomap for the family so take a copy with you to update it rather than starting from scratch.

Assessment explanatory notes		Consent form		Complaints procedure	
Direct work tools		Genogram		Eco Map	
Referral forms					

Demographics –If the family are known to the service or using the referral, make a note of the information you have for them and check with the family when you meet to make sure it is current and accurate.

Name		DOB		Gender		Disability	
Name		DOB		Gender		Disability	
Name		DOB		Gender		Disability	
Name		DOB		Gender		Disability	

Ethnicity	Language	Religion	Legal status

Further information (parental responsibility, child or parent with disability as identified by the service. Information about the family's *structure, culture, religion, ethnic origin* needs to be collected and analysed as the information could have significant bearing on their approach to parenting, child safety and impact the child.

Section Three: Explore the parents/carers/family's understanding of the concerns and the referral.

Section Four: Gathering and analysing the information for each child

This section allows you to gather information for about four children, so you may have to use copy pages if you need more). Information gathering should focus on strengths as well as difficulties. You can separate the areas below as appropriate.

(1) Health
(2) Education
(3) Emotional and Behavioural Development
(4) Identity
(5) Social Relationships
(6) Self-care skills
(7) Social presentation

Continuation of Section Four: Gathering and analysing the information for each child

Section Five: Parenting Capacity

This includes evidence of direct observations supplemented by information from other professionals, discussions parents and direct work and discussions with the child/ren.   Include analysis of strengths, difficulties and unmet needs – what if *anything is having a negative or positive impact on the child/ren.*

(1) Basic care
(2) Ensuring safety
(3)   Emotional warmth
(4) Stimulation
(5) Guidance and Boundaries
(6) Stability

Continuation of Section Five: Parenting Capacity

Section Six: Family and environmental factors

This section should include evidence from own observations and other sources. Consider adults in the home and around the child/ren who are considered to be or likely to be posting a risk of significant harm to the child/ren. Again topics can be combined or separated

(1) Family History and Functioning
(2) Wider Family and Significant Others
(3) Housing, Employment and Income
(4) Family's social integration/community resources
(5) Any current/historical social care involvement/services from other agencies

Continuation of Section Six: Family and Environmental Factors

Section Eight: Risks and Protective Factors

Section One: Preparation

Background - review the referral, management case directions, chronology, history of involvement and anything you feel will help you to understand the task ahead.

Section Two: The Initial or Assessment Home Visit

The first home visit to the family is your opportunity to collect significant facts about the family and get some of the formalities out of the way. In preparation for the visit, use the checklist below plus any other to make sure you have what you need. If there has been previous involvement, you might already have a genogram or ecomap for the family so take a copy with you to update it rather than starting from scratch.

Assessment explanatory notes		Consent form		Complaints procedure	
Direct work tools		Genogram		Eco Map	
Referral forms					

Demographics —If the family are known to the service or using the referral, make a note of the information you have for them and check with the family when you meet to make sure it is current and accurate.

Name		DOB		Gender		Disability	
Name		DOB		Gender		Disability	
Name		DOB		Gender		Disability	
Name		DOB		Gender		Disability	

Ethnicity	Language	Religion	Legal status

Further information (parental responsibility, child or parent with disability as identified by the service. Information about the family's *structure, culture, religion, ethnic origin* needs to be collected and analysed as the information could have significant bearing on their approach to parenting, child safety and impact the child.

Section Three: Explore the parents/carers/family's understanding of the concerns and the referral.

Section Four: Gathering and analysing the information for each child

This section allows you to gather information for about four children, so you may have to use copy pages if you need more). Information gathering should focus on strengths as well as difficulties. You can separate the areas below as appropriate.

(1) Health
(2) Education
(3) Emotional and Behavioural Development
(4) Identity
(5) Social Relationships
(6) Self-care skills
(7) Social presentation

Section Five: Parenting Capacity

This includes evidence of direct observations supplemented by information from other professionals, discussions parents and direct work and discussions with the child/ren.   Include analysis of strengths, difficulties and unmet needs – what if *anything is having a negative or positive impact on the child/ren.*

(1) Basic care
(2) Ensuring safety
(3)   Emotional warmth
(4) Stimulation
(5) Guidance and Boundaries
(6)   Stability

Continuation of Section Five: Parenting Capacity

Section Six: Family and environmental factors

This section should include evidence from own observations and other sources. Consider adults in the home and around the child/ren who are considered to be or likely to be posting a risk of significant harm to the child/ren. Again topics can be combined or separated

(1) Family History and Functioning
(2) Wider Family and Significant Others
(3) Housing, Employment and Income
(4) Family's social integration/community resources
(5) Any current/historical social care involvement/services from other agencies

Continuation of Section Six: Family and Environmental Factors

Section Seven: Views of All Parties

Section Eight: Risks and Protective Factors

Section One: Preparation

Background - *review the referral, management case directions, chronology, history of involvement and anything you feel will help you to understand the task ahead.*

Section Two: The Initial or Assessment Home Visit

The first home visit to the family is your opportunity to collect significant facts about the family and get some of the formalities out of the way. In preparation for the visit, use the checklist below plus any other to make sure you have what you need.   If there has been previous involvement, you might already have a genogram or ecomap for the family so take a copy with you to update it rather than starting from scratch.

Assessment explanatory notes		Consent form		Complaints procedure	
Direct work tools		Genogram		Eco Map	
Referral forms					

Demographics —If the family are known to the service or using the referral, make a note of the information you have for them and check with the family when you meet to make sure it is current and accurate.

Name		DOB		Gender		Disability	
Name		DOB		Gender		Disability	
Name		DOB		Gender		Disability	
Name		DOB		Gender		Disability	

Ethnicity	Language	Religion	Legal status

Further information (parental responsibility, child or parent with disability as identified by the service. Information about the family's *structure, culture, religion, ethnic origin* needs to be collected and analysed as the information could have significant bearing on their approach to parenting, child safety and impact the child.

Section Three: Explore the parents/carers/family's understanding of the concerns and the referral.

Section Four: Gathering and analysing the information for each child

This section allows you to gather information for about four children, so you may have to use copy pages if you need more). Information gathering should focus on strengths as well as difficulties.   You can separate the areas below as appropriate.

(1) Health
(2) Education
(3) Emotional and Behavioural Development
(4) Identity
(5)   Social Relationships
(6) Self-care skills
(7) Social presentation

Section Five: Parenting Capacity

This includes evidence of direct observations supplemented by information from other professionals, discussions parents and direct work and discussions with the child/ren. Include analysis of strengths, difficulties and unmet needs – what if *anything is having a negative or positive impact on the child/ren.*

(1) Basic care
(2) Ensuring safety
(3) Emotional warmth
(4) Stimulation
(5) Guidance and Boundaries
(6) Stability

Section Six: Family and environmental factors

This section should include evidence from own observations and other sources. Consider adults in the home and around the child/ren who are considered to be or likely to be posting a risk of significant harm to the child/ren. Again topics can be combined or separated

(1) Family History and Functioning
(2) Wider Family and Significant Others
(3) Housing, Employment and Income
(4) Family's social integration/community resources
(5) Any current/historical social care involvement/services from other agencies

Continuation of Section Six: Family and Environmental Factors

Section Eight: Risks and Protective Factors

Section One: Preparation

Background - *review the referral, management case directions, chronology, history of involvement and anything you feel will help you to understand the task ahead.*

Section Two: The Initial or Assessment Home Visit

The first home visit to the family is your opportunity to collect significant facts about the family and get some of the formalities out of the way. In preparation for the visit, use the checklist below plus any other to make sure you have what you need. If there has been previous involvement, you might already have a genogram or ecomap for the family so take a copy with you to update it rather than starting from scratch.

Assessment explanatory notes		Consent form		Complaints procedure	
Direct work tools		Genogram		Eco Map	
Referral forms					

Demographics –If the family are known to the service or using the referral, make a note of the information you have for them and check with the family when you meet to make sure it is current and accurate.

Name		DOB		Gender		Disability	
Name		DOB		Gender		Disability	
Name		DOB		Gender		Disability	
Name		DOB		Gender		Disability	

Ethnicity	Language	Religion	Legal status

Further information (parental responsibility, child or parent with disability as identified by the service. Information about the family's *structure, culture, religion, ethnic origin* needs to be collected and analysed as the information could have significant bearing on their approach to parenting, child safety and impact the child.

Section Three: Explore the parents/carers/family's understanding of the concerns and the referral.

Section Four: Gathering and analysing the information for each child

 This section allows you to gather information for about four children, so you may have to use copy pages
if you need more). Information gathering should focus on strengths as well as difficulties.   You can
separate the areas below as appropriate.

(1) Health
(2) Education
(3) Emotional and Behavioural Development
(4) Identity
(5)   Social Relationships
(6) Self-care skills
(7) Social presentation

Continuation of Section Four: Gathering and analysing the information for each child

Continuation of Section Four: Gathering and analysing the information for each child

Section Five: Parenting Capacity

This includes evidence of direct observations supplemented by information from other professionals, discussions parents and direct work and discussions with the child/ren.   Include analysis of strengths, difficulties and unmet needs – what if *anything is having a negative or positive impact on the child/ren.*

(1) Basic care
(2) Ensuring safety
(3)   Emotional warmth
(4) Stimulation
(5) Guidance and Boundaries
(6)   Stability

Continuation of Section Five: Parenting Capacity

Section Six: Family and environmental factors

This section should include evidence from own observations and other sources. Consider adults in the home and around the child/ren who are considered to be or likely to be posting a risk of significant harm to the child/ren. Again topics can be combined or separated

(1) Family History and Functioning
(2) Wider Family and Significant Others
(3) Housing, Employment and Income
(4) Family's social integration/community resources
(5) Any current/historical social care involvement/services from other agencies

Section Seven: Views of All Parties

Section Seven: Views of All Parties

Section Eight: Risks and Protective Factors

Section One: Preparation

Background - *review the referral, management case directions, chronology, history of involvement and anything you feel will help you to understand the task ahead.*

Section Two: The Initial or Assessment Home Visit

The first home visit to the family is your opportunity to collect significant facts about the family and get some of the formalities out of the way. In preparation for the visit, use the checklist below plus any other to make sure you have what you need. If there has been previous involvement, you might already have a genogram or ecomap for the family so take a copy with you to update it rather than starting from scratch.

Assessment explanatory notes		Consent form		Complaints procedure	
Direct work tools		Genogram		Eco Map	
Referral forms					

Demographics –If the family are known to the service or using the referral, make a note of the information you have for them and check with the family when you meet to make sure it is current and accurate.

Name		DOB		Gender		Disability	
Name		DOB		Gender		Disability	
Name		DOB		Gender		Disability	
Name		DOB		Gender		Disability	

Ethnicity	Language	Religion	Legal status

Further information (parental responsibility, child or parent with disability as identified by the service. Information about the family's *structure, culture, religion, ethnic origin* needs to be collected and analysed as the information could have significant bearing on their approach to parenting, child safety and impact the child.

Section Four: Gathering and analysing the information for each child

This section allows you to gather information for about four children, so you may have to use copy pages if you need more). Information gathering should focus on strengths as well as difficulties.   You can separate the areas below as appropriate.

(1) Health
(2) Education
(3) Emotional and Behavioural Development
(4) Identity
(5)   Social Relationships
(6) Self-care skills
(7) Social presentation

Section Five: Parenting Capacity

This includes evidence of direct observations supplemented by information from other professionals, discussions parents and direct work and discussions with the child/ren.   Include analysis of strengths, difficulties and unmet needs – what if *anything is having a negative or positive impact on the child/ren.*

(1) Basic care
(2) Ensuring safety
(3)   Emotional warmth
(4) Stimulation
(5) Guidance and Boundaries
(6)   Stability

Section Six: Family and environmental factors

This section should include evidence from own observations and other sources. Consider adults in the home and around the child/ren who are considered to be or likely to be posting a risk of significant harm to the child/ren. Again topics can be combined or separated

(1) Family History and Functioning
(2) Wider Family and Significant Others
(3) Housing, Employment and Income
(4) Family's social integration/community resources
(5) Any current/historical social care involvement/services from other agencies

Continuation of Section Six: Family and Environmental Factors

Section Seven: Views of All Parties

Section Eight: Risks and Protective Factors

Section One: Preparation

Background - review the referral, management case directions, chronology, history of involvement and anything you feel will help you to understand the task ahead.

Section Two: The Initial or Assessment Home Visit

The first home visit to the family is your opportunity to collect significant facts about the family and get some of the formalities out of the way. In preparation for the visit, use the checklist below plus any other to make sure you have what you need. If there has been previous involvement, you might already have a genogram or ecomap for the family so take a copy with you to update it rather than starting from scratch.

Assessment explanatory notes		Consent form		Complaints procedure	
Direct work tools		Genogram		Eco Map	
Referral forms					

Demographics –If the family are known to the service or using the referral, make a note of the information you have for them and check with the family when you meet to make sure it is current and accurate.

Name		DOB		Gender		Disability	
Name		DOB		Gender		Disability	
Name		DOB		Gender		Disability	
Name		DOB		Gender		Disability	

Ethnicity	Language	Religion	Legal status

Further information (parental responsibility, child or parent with disability as identified by the service. Information about the family's *structure, culture, religion, ethnic origin* needs to be collected and analysed as the information could have significant bearing on their approach to parenting, child safety and impact the child.

Section Three: Explore the parents/carers/family's understanding of the concerns and the referral.

Section Four: Gathering and analysing the information for each child

 This section allows you to gather information for about four children, so you may have to use copy pages if you need more). Information gathering should focus on strengths as well as difficulties.   You can separate the areas below as appropriate.

(1) Health
(2) Education
(3) Emotional and Behavioural Development
(4) Identity
(5)   Social Relationships
(6) Self-care skills
(7) Social presentation

Continuation of Section Four: Gathering and analysing the information for each child

Section Five: Parenting Capacity

This includes evidence of direct observations supplemented by information from other professionals, discussions parents and direct work and discussions with the child/ren. Include analysis of strengths, difficulties and unmet needs – what if *anything is having a negative or positive impact on the child/ren.*

(1) Basic care
(2) Ensuring safety
(3) Emotional warmth
(4) Stimulation
(5) Guidance and Boundaries
(6) Stability

Continuation of Section Five: Parenting Capacity

Section Six: Family and environmental factors

This section should include evidence from own observations and other sources. Consider adults in the home and around the child/ren who are considered to be or likely to be posting a risk of significant harm to the child/ren. Again topics can be combined or separated

(1) Family History and Functioning
(2) Wider Family and Significant Others
(3) Housing, Employment and Income
(4) Family's social integration/community resources
(5) Any current/historical social care involvement/services from other agencies

Section Eight: Risks and Protective Factors

Section One: Preparation

Background - *review the referral, management case directions, chronology, history of involvement and anything you feel will help you to understand the task ahead.*

Section Two: The Initial or Assessment Home Visit

The first home visit to the family is your opportunity to collect significant facts about the family and get some of the formalities out of the way. In preparation for the visit, use the checklist below plus any other to make sure you have what you need. If there has been previous involvement, you might already have a genogram or ecomap for the family so take a copy with you to update it rather than starting from scratch.

Assessment explanatory notes		Consent form		Complaints procedure	
Direct work tools		Genogram		Eco Map	
Referral forms					

Demographics –If the family are known to the service or using the referral, make a note of the information you have for them and check with the family when you meet to make sure it is current and accurate.

Name		DOB		Gender		Disability	
Name		DOB		Gender		Disability	
Name		DOB		Gender		Disability	
Name		DOB		Gender		Disability	

Ethnicity	Language	Religion	Legal status

Further information (parental responsibility, child or parent with disability as identified by the service. Information about the family's *structure, culture, religion, ethnic origin* needs to be collected and analysed as the information could have significant bearing on their approach to parenting, child safety and impact the child.

Section Four: Gathering and analysing the information for each child

This section allows you to gather information for about four children, so you may have to use copy pages if you need more). Information gathering should focus on strengths as well as difficulties. You can separate the areas below as appropriate.

(1) Health
(2) Education
(3) Emotional and Behavioural Development
(4) Identity
(5) Social Relationships
(6) Self-care skills
(7) Social presentation

Section Five: Parenting Capacity

This includes evidence of direct observations supplemented by information from other professionals, discussions parents and direct work and discussions with the child/ren.   Include analysis of strengths, difficulties and unmet needs – what if *anything is having a negative or positive impact on the child/ren.*

(1) Basic care
(2) Ensuring safety
(3) Emotional warmth
(4) Stimulation
(5) Guidance and Boundaries
(6) Stability

Section Six: Family and environmental factors

This section should include evidence from own observations and other sources. Consider adults in the home and around the child/ren who are considered to be or likely to be posting a risk of significant harm to the child/ren. Again topics can be combined or separated

(1) Family History and Functioning
(2) Wider Family and Significant Others
(3) Housing, Employment and Income
(4) Family's social integration/community resources
(5) Any current/historical social care involvement/services from other agencies

Section Eight: Risks and Protective Factors

Section One: Preparation

Background - review the referral, management case directions, chronology, history of involvement and anything you feel will help you to understand the task ahead.

Section Two: The Initial or Assessment Home Visit

The first home visit to the family is your opportunity to collect significant facts about the family and get some of the formalities out of the way. In preparation for the visit, use the checklist below plus any other to make sure you have what you need. If there has been previous involvement, you might already have a genogram or ecomap for the family so take a copy with you to update it rather than starting from scratch.

Assessment explanatory notes		Consent form		Complaints procedure	
Direct work tools		Genogram		Eco Map	
Referral forms					

Demographics —If the family are known to the service or using the referral, make a note of the information you have for them and check with the family when you meet to make sure it is current and accurate.

Name		DOB		Gender		Disability	
Name		DOB		Gender		Disability	
Name		DOB		Gender		Disability	
Name		DOB		Gender		Disability	

Ethnicity	Language	Religion	Legal status

Further information (parental responsibility, child or parent with disability as identified by the service. Information about the family's ***structure, culture, religion, ethnic origin*** needs to be collected and analysed as the information could have significant bearing on their approach to parenting, child safety and impact the child.

Section Three: Explore the parents/carers/family's understanding of the concerns and the referral.

Section Four: Gathering and analysing the information for each child

This section allows you to gather information for about four children, so you may have to use copy pages if you need more). Information gathering should focus on strengths as well as difficulties. You can separate the areas below as appropriate.

(1) Health
(2) Education
(3) Emotional and Behavioural Development
(4) Identity
(5) Social Relationships
(6) Self-care skills
(7) Social presentation

Continuation of Section Four: Gathering and analysing the information for each child

Section Five: Parenting Capacity

This includes evidence of direct observations supplemented by information from other professionals, discussions parents and direct work and discussions with the child/ren. Include analysis of strengths, difficulties and unmet needs – what if *anything is having a negative or positive impact on the child/ren.*

(1) Basic care
(2) Ensuring safety
(3) Emotional warmth
(4) Stimulation
(5) Guidance and Boundaries
(6) Stability

Section Six: Family and environmental factors

This section should include evidence from own observations and other sources. Consider adults in the home and around the child/ren who are considered to be or likely to be posting a risk of significant harm to the child/ren. Again topics can be combined or separated

(1) Family History and Functioning
(2) Wider Family and Significant Others
(3) Housing, Employment and Income
(4) Family's social integration/community resources
(5) Any current/historical social care involvement/services from other agencies

Section Seven: Views of All Parties

Section Eight: Risks and Protective Factors

Section One: Preparation

Background - *review the referral, management case directions, chronology, history of involvement and anything you feel will help you to understand the task ahead.*

Section Two: The Initial or Assessment Home Visit

The first home visit to the family is your opportunity to collect significant facts about the family and get some of the formalities out of the way. In preparation for the visit, use the checklist below plus any other to make sure you have what you need. If there has been previous involvement, you might already have a genogram or ecomap for the family so take a copy with you to update it rather than starting from scratch.

Assessment explanatory notes		Consent form		Complaints procedure	
Direct work tools		Genogram		Eco Map	
Referral forms					

Demographics –If the family are known to the service or using the referral, make a note of the information you have for them and check with the family when you meet to make sure it is current and accurate.

Name		DOB		Gender		Disability	
Name		DOB		Gender		Disability	
Name		DOB		Gender		Disability	
Name		DOB		Gender		Disability	

Ethnicity	Language	Religion	Legal status

Further information (parental responsibility, child or parent with disability as identified by the service. Information about the family's *structure, culture, religion, ethnic origin* needs to be collected and analysed as the information could have significant bearing on their approach to parenting, child safety and impact the child.

Section Three: Explore the parents/carers/family's understanding of the concerns and the referral.

Section Four: Gathering and analysing the information for each child

This section allows you to gather information for about four children, so you may have to use copy pages if you need more). Information gathering should focus on strengths as well as difficulties.   You can separate the areas below as appropriate.

(1) Health
(2) Education
(3) Emotional and Behavioural Development
(4) Identity
(5)   Social Relationships
(6) Self-care skills
(7) Social presentation

Continuation of Section Four: Gathering and analysing the information for each child

Section Five: Parenting Capacity

This includes evidence of direct observations supplemented by information from other professionals, discussions parents and direct work and discussions with the child/ren.   Include analysis of strengths, difficulties and unmet needs – what if *anything is having a negative or positive impact on the child/ren.*

(1) Basic care
(2) Ensuring safety
(3) Emotional warmth
(4) Stimulation
(5) Guidance and Boundaries
(6) Stability

Continuation of Section Five: Parenting Capacity

Section Six: Family and environmental factors

This section should include evidence from own observations and other sources. Consider adults in the home and around the child/ren who are considered to be or likely to be posting a risk of significant harm to the child/ren. Again topics can be combined or separated

(1) Family History and Functioning
(2) Wider Family and Significant Others
(3) Housing, Employment and Income
(4) Family's social integration/community resources
(5) Any current/historical social care involvement/services from other agencies

Section Eight: Risks and Protective Factors

Section One: Preparation

Background - review the referral, management case directions, chronology, history of involvement and anything you feel will help you to understand the task ahead.

Section Two: The Initial or Assessment Home Visit

The first home visit to the family is your opportunity to collect significant facts about the family and get some of the formalities out of the way. In preparation for the visit, use the checklist below plus any other to make sure you have what you need. If there has been previous involvement, you might already have a genogram or ecomap for the family so take a copy with you to update it rather than starting from scratch.

Assessment explanatory notes		Consent form		Complaints procedure	
Direct work tools		Genogram		Eco Map	
Referral forms					

Demographics – If the family are known to the service or using the referral, make a note of the information you have for them and check with the family when you meet to make sure it is current and accurate.

Name		DOB		Gender		Disability	
Name		DOB		Gender		Disability	
Name		DOB		Gender		Disability	
Name		DOB		Gender		Disability	

Ethnicity	Language	Religion	Legal status

Further information (parental responsibility, child or parent with disability as identified by the service. Information about the family's *structure, culture, religion, ethnic origin* needs to be collected and analysed as the information could have significant bearing on their approach to parenting, child safety and impact the child.

Section Three: Explore the parents/carers/family's understanding of the concerns and the referral.

Section Four: Gathering and analysing the information for each child

This section allows you to gather information for about four children, so you may have to use copy pages if you need more). Information gathering should focus on strengths as well as difficulties. You can separate the areas below as appropriate.

(1) Health
(2) Education
(3) Emotional and Behavioural Development
(4) Identity
(5) Social Relationships
(6) Self-care skills
(7) Social presentation

Continuation of Section Four: Gathering and analysing the information for each child

Section Five: Parenting Capacity

This includes evidence of direct observations supplemented by information from other professionals, discussions parents and direct work and discussions with the child/ren. Include analysis of strengths, difficulties and unmet needs – what if *anything is having a negative or positive impact on the child/ren.*

(1) Basic care
(2) Ensuring safety
(3) Emotional warmth
(4) Stimulation
(5) Guidance and Boundaries
(6) Stability

Section Six: Family and environmental factors

This section should include evidence from own observations and other sources. Consider adults in the home and around the child/ren who are considered to be or likely to be posting a risk of significant harm to the child/ren. Again topics can be combined or separated

(1) Family History and Functioning
(2) Wider Family and Significant Others
(3) Housing, Employment and Income
(4) Family's social integration/community resources
(5) Any current/historical social care involvement/services from other agencies

Continuation of Section Six: Family and Environmental Factors

Section Seven: Views of All Parties

Section Seven: Views of All Parties

Section Eight: Risks and Protective Factors